A GUIDE TO THE CHARACTERS OF

Jim Henson's

THE DARK CRYSTAL

AGE OF RESISTANCE

HEROES OF THE RESISTANCE

PENGUIN YOUNG READERS LICENSES
An Imprint of Penguin Random House LLC, New York

Stock images: Shutterstock

Published in 2019 by Penguin Young Readers Licenses, an imprint of Penguin Random House LLC, New York. Manufactured in China.

Visit us online at www.penguinrandomhouse.com.

ISBN 9780593095393   10 9 8 7 6 5 4 3 2 1

A GUIDE TO THE CHARACTERS OF

Jim Henson's

THE DARK CRYSTAL

Age of Resistance

HEROES OF THE RESISTANCE

BY J. M. LEE

Table of Contents

Deatea. Deratea. Kidakida. Arugaru . . .

Hear it, don't you? Hear the song of our world?
The song of Thra! It calls. Full of pain. Corrupted.
Broken. Darkened.

I am Aughra the Helix-Horned. Many trine ago, Thra had
no voice with which to speak. No eyes with which to see.
And so I was born. I wandered the awakening world
and learned the language of every flower and every
stone. I came to know the song then: *Deatea. Deratea.
Kidakida. Arugaru.*

I watched as life on Thra flourished. Gentle Gelfling rose
from the soil and blossomed. They formed seven great
clans and lived in peace with one another and the world
around them.

Then the Skeksis came. Intelligent and ambitious,
gregarious and manipulative. They unevenly bestowed
their favor upon the Gelfling, driving rifts of rivalry and
suspicion among the clans. Seeking ultimate power, they
broke the Crystal that is the heart of our world. Changed

its light to darkness. Used their machines on the Crystal and contorted it. Instead of giving life, now the Crystal takes. What was once the Crystal of Truth is now the Dark Crystal.

The Crystal veins that spread throughout Thra became darkened. The flora and fauna that were sustained by the Crystal became darkened, too. All because of what the Skeksis had done.

Thra had to do something. Aughra had to do something. So, we listened . . .

Can you hear its song now? The Crystal's cry for help? Yes, you can. I can see that you can, little Gelfling. You can hear its haunting song in your heart. You heard it call out to you, and you replied. That is why you are here, in our dreamspace. Where all the Gelfling of the resistance have gathered.

Know their faces, Gelfling! Know their names! Know their songs! So you may unite the seven clans and resist the Skeksis!

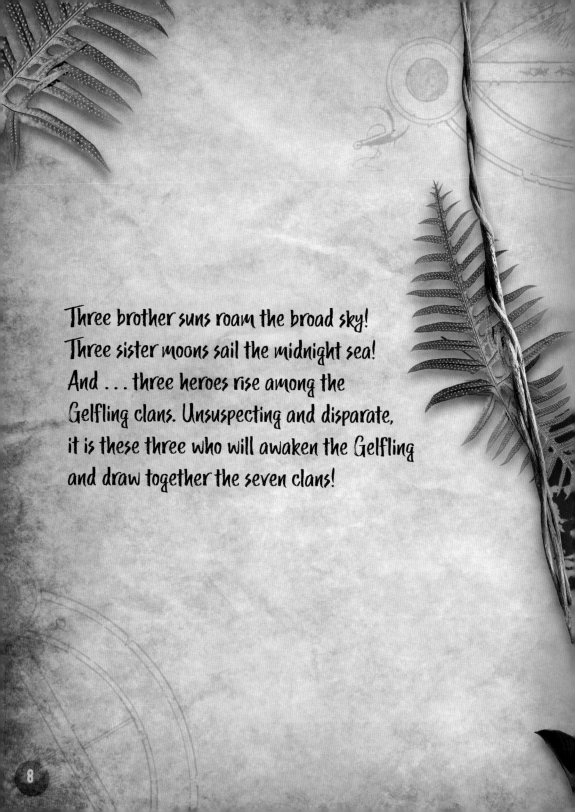

Three brother suns roam the broad sky!
Three sister moons sail the midnight sea!
And . . . three heroes rise among the
Gelfling clans. Unsuspecting and disparate,
it is these three who will awaken the Gelfling
and draw together the seven clans!

HEROES OF THE RESISTANCE

RIAN

GOAL:
To tell the Gelfling that
the Skeksis Lords have
betrayed them

CLAN:
Stonewood

HOMETOWN:
Stone-in-the-Wood

STORY

Rian was a guard at the Castle of the Crystal, where he served the Skeksis Lords along with the other Gelfling guards. When he and his friends Mira and Gurjin went hunting a rogue Silk Spitter in the catacombs beneath the castle, they discovered a horrible secret: Emperor skekSo and the other Skeksis had corrupted the Crystal of Truth, transforming it into the Dark Crystal. Using its awful power, they drained Mira's life Essence into a glowing liquid that they drank like wine.

Knowing he had to warn the other Gelfling of the Skeksis' awful treachery, Rian stole the vial of Essence as proof and escaped the castle, fleeing for his life.

After being spurned by Maudra Fara of the Stonewood, Rian hopes to bring his only proof—the vial of Mira's Essence—to the Gelfling All-Maudra, Mayrin. But reaching her is difficult, especially when he's being hunted by both the deadly Skeksis Hunter and by his own father, Ordon.

PERSONALITY

Growing up as the son of the Captain of the Guard, Rian never questioned his future. But after fleeing the castle, and burdened with the Skeksis' terrible secret, Rian knows his dreams of taking after his father can be no more. Marked by the Skeksis as a traitor and a fugitive, he must find a new purpose in the turbulent, dangerous new world he has uncovered.

DESCRIPTION

Rian has dark hair broken by streaks of blue, gray eyes, and an athletic physique. As befits a guard serving the Castle of the Crystal, he is comfortable in a Landstrider's saddle or aboard a Skeksis carriage. He is also skilled with many weapons, though he favors the spear and sword. But this captain's son is not all brawn; he's a fine hand at the lute if given the chance.

THE VIAL OF ESSENCE

After witnessing the Skeksis' Essence-draining machinery in action, Rian stole a vial of Essence in the hopes that it might be proof enough to convince the other Gelfling that he is telling the truth.

BREA

GOAL:
To learn the meaning of the Aureyal and set things right among the seven clans

CLAN:
Vapra

HOMETOWN:
Ha'rar

STORY

Brea is the youngest daughter of All-Maudra Mayrin, the leader of the Vapra clan. She grew up in snowy Ha'rar, a northern village that faces the expansive Silver Sea. When Brea's curiosity and keen intelligence brought her to doubt the Skeksis' rule over the Gelfling, she dove headlong into a search for answers—against her mother's wishes. What she found was a long-buried chain of secrets, the end of which may lead her to the truth about the Skeksis Lords.

Brea knows that pursuing the truth will not be easy. The Gelfling have settled into the system of clans and leadership of the Skeksis. Brea knows in her heart that clearing the dust from the old songs and reconnecting the seven clans may be the only way to lead the Gelfling out from under the Skeksis' shadow.

PERSONALITY

Brea is enamored of the songs of the past. She loves the oldest and dustiest books, and has studied many old scripts just so she can read them. She has a particular love for and interest in the stories that explain how things came to be the way they are today. While her two sisters, Seladon and Tavra, spend most of their time in the Citadel throne room and Paladin barracks, respectively, Brea can usually be found in the Vapran library with her nose buried in a dusty tome.

DESCRIPTION

Brea has pale skin, silver hair, and iridescent wings, and is often dressed in the traditional colors of a Vapran princess. Though she is not very skilled in combat, her mind and memory are brimming with knowledge both from the books she's read in the library and from the time she's spent with her mother in the Citadel. Most formidable, however, is her ability to persuade with words thanks to her raw honesty and practiced poise. Perhaps all her lessons with her mother and sisters didn't go to waste!

THE AUREYAL

Brea saw this mystical three-pointed symbol in the library, when it appeared in a brilliant flash of supernatural wind and light. Though many symbols are used in Gelfling writing, it is one that Brea has never seen before. Its shape seems to imply the cosmology of Thra and its three suns. What could it mean?

DEET

GOAL:
To travel to Ha'rar to tell the All-Maudra about the darkening

CLAN:
Grottan

HOMETOWN:
Domrak

STORY

Deet comes from Domrak, a village in the Caves of Grot. She spent most of her time tending to the Nurloc herds that grazed in the deepest parts of the caves. But even the hidden caves were not safe from the darkening. The Nurlocs, usually gentle and kind, were enraged. They attacked, and Deet fell even farther into the caves. When she awoke, she found herself face-to-face with an ancient stone tree. In a psychic dreamfast, the tree told her of the dark presence seeping out of the Castle of the Crystal. When Deet told Maudra Argot and the other Grottan Gelfling what had happened, they knew what she had to do. Deet was sent to the world above the caves to find help from the All-Maudra and the other Gelfling clans.

PERSONALITY

Deet always looks on the bright side, holding on to hope even in the face of the great challenges she encounters. Perhaps more than her friends, she has an affinity for the creatures of Thra. She is creative and kind, eager to overcome adversity and bring out the best in everyone. Sometimes, though, Deet's willingness to help others and heal the pain she sees around her can become overwhelming. If it means saving the rest of the Gelfling and Thra, Deet may find herself asking how far she would go if she could protect the world she cares about. Though Deet is not yet confident in her ability to bear her own torch, she strives to grow and to use her flame to light the torches of others.

DESCRIPTION

Deet is small, even for a Gelfling, and very nimble. She learned to fly in the underground ravines near Domrak, and readily applies her deft agility to flying topside. Though her dark eyes allow her to see in pitch black, they are sensitive in daylight at first.

THE DARKENING

Crystal veins, originating from, the Crystal of Truth in the Skeksis' castle, spread throughout Thra and deliver life to all things. Normally clear and bright, the Crystal veins of Thra have become ill. In their blight, they turn dark and purple—contact with them causes madness and rage in the usually peaceful creatures of Thra.

DREAMFASTING

When Gelfling choose to open their hearts to one another, they can *dreamfast*—by psychically connecting with one another through the touch of hands, they are able to share memories and thoughts. Dreamfasting is very intimate, as it requires Gelfling to be vulnerable with one another and to share their secrets.

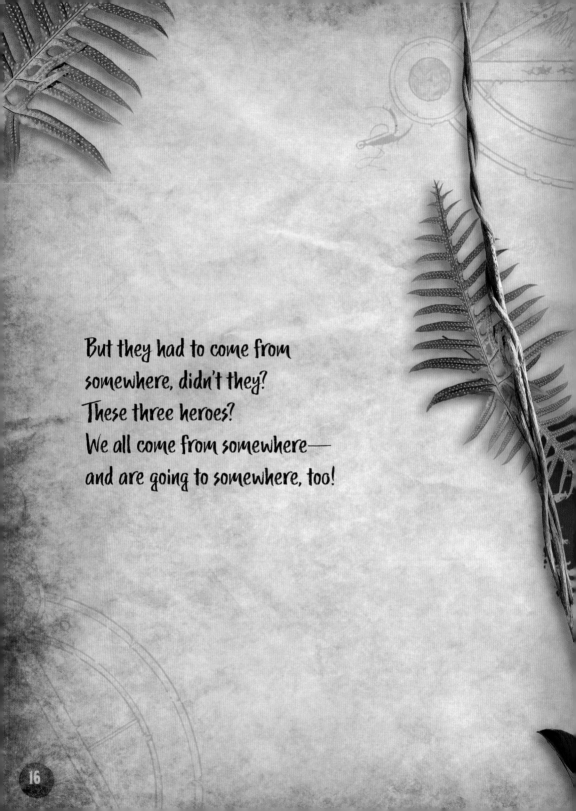

But they had to come from
somewhere, didn't they?
These three heroes?
We all come from somewhere—
and are going to somewhere, too!

Gelfling Friends and Family

Rian's Friends and Family:
At the
Castle
of the Crystal

Rian's journey to save the Gelfling begins on the edge of the Endless Forest, in a castle that dominates the horizon. The Castle of the Crystal, made of blackened stone and shaped like a claw. In the beginning, the Gelfling served here by choice. Loved the Skeksis, they did. Loved and respected. Because the Gelfling did not yet know the truth . . .

MIRA

CLAN:
Vapra

HOMETOWN:
Ha'rar

Brave and fun-loving, Mira is easily one of the most capable of the Castle Guards. She is fearless and a born leader, often the first to jump to the rescue when someone is in need of help. When she and Rian see a Silk Spitter on castle grounds, Mira knows right away that they should go after it—even if it might go against the wishes of the Captain of the Guard.

MIRA AND RIAN

Love can blossom even in the barracks of the Castle Guard. Mira knew Rian had feelings for her long before he said anything. When she realized he was too nervous, she took the lead and kissed him first.

GURJIN

CLAN:
Drenchen

HOMETOWN:
Great Smerth

Gurjin is the son of Maudra Laesid, the leader of the Drenchen clan. While his twin sister remained in the Swamp of Sog, training to become the next Drenchen Maudra, Gurjin left home to find his fortune as a guard at the Castle of the Crystal. Though Drenchen are not warmly welcomed among the Gelfling outside the swamp, Gurjin was determined to win everyone over. And he did! Now a favorite among the Castle Guards, Gurjin gets along with others easily thanks to his agreeable personality and sense of humor. While he might seem reluctant to take on too much responsibility at first, once committed, he is steadfast and unbreakable.

GURJIN AND RIAN

Gurjin became quick friends with Rian while they were serving as guards together. This connection would later lead Gurjin to join Rian and the other Gelfling in the resistance against the Skeksis.

ORDON

CLAN:
Stonewood

HOMETOWN:
Stone-in-the-Wood

ORDON AND RIAN

Ordon is a stern captain and an even stricter father to Rian. He believes that the way to success is through honor and steadfast responsibility for one's actions, values that he has tried to impress on his son. But it can't be denied that as a youth, Ordon had a rebellious streak—one that he sees in Rian.

Rian's father, Ordon, fought alongside the Skeksis in the Arathim Wars as a young Stonewood before coming to serve the Skeksis at the castle. After many years of hard work and unfaltering service, he eventually rose through the ranks to become Captain of the Guard. He is dutiful and traditional, with no doubt as to the Skeksis Lords' motives or true natures.

When the rumors begin that his son, Rian, may be responsible for the death of another guard, Ordon doesn't know what to think. He is loyal to the Skeksis, but he knows in his heart that Rian would never do such a thing. Blindly trusting the Skeksis instead of his own son, Ordon pursues Rian, determined to bring him back to the castle.

CASTLE GUARDS

Gelfling, both male and female, from almost every clan serve at the Castle of the Crystal. Their duties include regular patrol on the castle grounds; training and servicing the Armaligs, Landstriders, and other creatures; and repairing and maintaining the castle architecture itself. While the Castle of the Crystal is one of the few locations where many Gelfling of different clans intermingle, the Skeksis secretly make sure that their communities beyond the castle remain divided.

BREA'S FRIENDS AND FAMILY: IN HA'RAR, THE VAPRAN CAPITAL

Brea hails from the north, facing the Silver Sea: Ha'rar.
Here, in the height of glamour, stands the Citadel.
The throne from where Brea's mother, the All-Maudra,
rules, blinded by the shining light of the Skeksis.

SELADON

CLAN:
Vapra

HOMETOWN:
Ha'rar

Brea's oldest sister, Seladon, is first in line to inherit the All-Maudra's Living Crown. She is proud and extremely serious about her role as princess, determined to one day lead as confidently as her mother. Thus, all her efforts are focused on becoming the next All-Maudra and continuing the Vapran legacy of walking in the light of the Skeksis' favor.

Sometimes, this fixation on her role can be expressed as insensitive rivalry, as Seladon can be very critical of her sisters and those around her. She has high expectations, both for her family and for the many Gelfling who look up to and honor them. However, Seladon has much to learn about the world outside of Ha'rar, where her Maudra training will truly be put to the test.

SELADON AND BREA

Even though Seladon is the heir to the All-Maudra's Living Crown, she still can't let go of the idea that Brea is their mother's favorite. Because of this, she and Brea do not often get along. The constant quest for their mother's love motivates both of these sisters— sometimes threatening to drive them apart.

TAVRA

CLAN:
Vapra

HOMETOWN:
Ha'rar

TAVRA AND BREA

Tavra has a soft spot for her younger sister, Brea. She understands Brea's passion for justice and the truth, but she also knows Brea must learn what it means to be a Vapran princess if she's going to be able to harness that passion.

Tavra is All-Maudra Mayrin's stern middle child. She is a loyal and serious soldier, dividing her time between aiding her mother in the Citadel and training the Vapran Paladins who protect Ha'rar. Among the Paladins, she is a skilled tactician and tracker, as well as an expert sword handler. Among her family, she is often the peacekeeper. She believes in the best aspects of her sisters and her mother, even when they don't see eye-to-eye, and does her best to mediate during her family's not-infrequent confrontations. Although Tavra has no intention of ever becoming All-Maudra, her even-keeled personality and righteous confidence gain the trust of everyone she meets.

LORE

ORIGIN:
Unknown

Lore slept for hundreds of trine buried beneath the All-Maudra's throne room. He is a timeless stone messenger characterized by the ability to withstand the elements of nature. Lore's tireless patience makes him ideal for delivering important messages over long distances of both geography and time.

A secret message was stored inside Lore's ancient body—and that message was finally released by Brea when she discovered the secret chamber where Lore waited.

Who left this message, and what does it mean? Brea can only hope she will be able to find out!

DEET'S FRIENDS AND FAMILY: IN THE CAVES OF GROT

But all heroes don't come from castles and citadels, do they? No! Some, like Deet, come from the shadows. From the caves. From the deep, secret places, far away from others. Yes. Because those that come from the dark are not afraid of it.

LATH'N, MITJAN, AND BOBB'N

THE SANCTUARY TREE

CLAN:
Grottan

HOMETOWN:
Domrak

Deet's fathers, Lath'N and Mitjan, live in Domrak, along with Deet's baby brother, Bobb'N. They taught Deet everything they know about tending to the Nurlocs that live in the Grottan caves. They also taught her everything they know about the world that exists outside the caves—which, unfortunately, is very little. Saying goodbye to Deet and sending her out of the caves and into the bright world outside was no easy task.

The Sanctuary Tree, a large tree that grows in the mountains, has two faces: a pink-petaled tree that enjoys the sun of the surface, and an underground, inverted stone tree that dangles deep in the Caves of Grot. The Sanctuary Tree, like all the seven sacred trees, is deeply connected to Thra, to Aughra, and to the Gelfling. It has seen hundreds of trine, both atop the mountains and below them, and when Aughra comes looking for answers, the Sanctuary Tree—as it always has—does its best to give.

But beyond its gentle appearance, the Sanctuary Tree bears a silent pain. Since the darkening of the Crystal, the tree has been absorbing the encroaching darkness, protecting the Gelfling that live in the caves. So far, it has endured, but for how long?

HUP

HOMETOWN:
Sami Thicket

HUP AND DEET

Hup meets Deet when she first adventures into the world outside the Caves of Grot. Together, they fend off a violent Silk Spitter. Hup is especially protective of Deet, who can be a bit naive when it comes to the "daylighter" world. Still, Hup is charmed by Deet's enthusiasm, and he will do anything to protect her.

There has never been a Podling Paladin among the Vapran ranks, but that doesn't stop this Podling cook from dreaming big. Hup decided to make the trek to Ha'rar wielding only a wooden spoon, determined to become the first Podling Paladin to serve the All-Maudra. Hup is earnest and brave despite the often troubling things he's seen and overcome. His experiences have left him somewhat jaded, but with all the more motivation to join the Vapran Paladins as a knight of honor and justice.

Hup understands the Gelfling language, though he's more comfortable speaking in Podling. This changes when he meets Deet, though, as it becomes clear that he will need to become proficient in the Gelfling tongue if he wants to help his friends and become a Paladin in Ha'rar.

GELFLING ALLIES

Our heroes rose to the task of resisting the Skeksis.
But they could not do it by themselves. Though at first it
seemed they walked alone, the stars aligned above and
their paths converged below. Other torches flickered
through the dark! The fires of resistance!

CLAN:
Vapra

HOMETOWN:
Ha'rar

THE LIBRARIAN AND PLUFF'M

Keeping and organizing the unending tomes within the Vapran library is no small task, and one that falls to the elder librarian and his Pluff'M familiar. Together, the two spend every day sorting, stocking, and reshelving the scrolls, scripts, tablets, and books. Though it's rumored the librarian saw more wild and adventurous days in his youth sailing with the Sifan Elder Cadia, that curiosity has settled in his old age. Now, he spends most of his time maintaining the library and the status quo, hoping to keep Brea out of trouble. Perhaps, one day, a worthy cause will reawaken the fierceness of his youth . . .

ONICA

CLAN:
Sifa

HOMETOWN:
Cera-Na

Onica is a Sifan Far-Dreamer—
a soothsayer in touch with the
hidden ways of Thra. In spite
of her youth, she is intuitive
and mystical beyond her years,
well versed in symbology
and the art of making potions
and salves after many trine of
apprenticeship. Onica has
always been able to hear the
Crystal singing in its broken
melody, but it has never
frightened her. In fact, it only
strengthens her resolve to do
whatever is necessary to make
things right . . . even if it goes
against the traditions of her
elders.

ONICA AND BREA

At first, Onica seems to be
interested only in what Brea
can pay in exchange for Sifan
wisdom. But beyond her
mysterious front, Onica is
practical and earnest. Later,
when things become more
dangerous, Onica's surprising
protectiveness of Brea belies
her enigmatic facade . . .
leading Brea to wonder if
there might be more to Onica
than meets the eye.

ELDER CADIA

THE DAUDRAN AND THE ORDER OF LESSER SERVICE

CLAN:
Sifa
HOMETOWN:
Cera-Na

CLAN:
Vapra
HOMETOWN:
Ha'rar

Elder Cadia is a renowned soothsayer among the Sifa who frequent the Ha'rar port, trading his wisdom for shining trinkets offered by his Vapran clients. His expertise is in interpreting the symbols and signs found within both dreams and the waking world, although he is a skilled apothecary when the need arises. He is superstitious and can be fatalistic, especially if he believes the portents of his visions to be unavoidable. All Sifa know destiny is final! So what would be the point in pursuing a prophecy of doom, except to find oneself in imminent danger? In his opinion, such knowledge might be best forgotten . . .

The Daudran is the staunch head of the Ha'rar chapter of the Order of Lesser Service, an organization that puts young, wayward Gelfling to work improving their community by performing tasks that others might prefer not to do. Tasks include pre-chewing roots for orphaned Nebries and bathing Podlings. As a youth, the Daudran might have had dreams of becoming a Paladin or serving the All-Maudra within the Citadel, but running the Lesser Service has become his present and, most likely, his remaining future.

JUNI

CLAN:
Vapra

HOMETOWN:
Ha'rar

This peppy Gelfling is a fast talker who loves to overshare, so it didn't take long for Brea to find out this is her third time with the Order of Lesser Service. And all because of her infatuation with a Spriton boy! Will she learn her lesson and stay out of the Order after this time around? More importantly . . . will she ever connect with her crush?

NAIA

CLAN:
Drenchen

HOMETOWN:
Great Smerth

NAIA AND GURJIN

Growing up as twins wasn't easy, though Naia and Gurjin were more similar than different as children. When Gurjin left to become a guard at the castle, the two began to grow apart. But that doesn't mean they won't unite against the Skeksis—both as Drenchen and as inseparable siblings.

Naia is the heroine of the *Dark Crystal* young adult tie-in novels *Shadows of the Dark Crystal* and *Flames of the Dark Crystal*.

Naia is Gurjin's twin sister and the eldest daughter of the Drenchen Maudra, Laesid. Naia leaves the Swamp of Sog, where the Drenchen clan live, when she hears that Gurjin has gone missing—and that it may be the fault of a Stonewood soldier named Rian. But after Naia finally meets Rian and hears his story, she changes her approach and becomes one of his strongest allies.

Naia is hard-willed and excellent in combat, a strong leader and incalculably loyal once her trust is earned. As the next Drenchen Maudra, she is also well versed in politics and diplomacy—even if her delivery of such things may be rough around the edges.

Both headstrong leaders, Naia and Rian can sometimes find themselves at odds. But in the end, they both care deeply about rallying the Gelfling and resisting the Skeksis.

KYLAN

CLAN:
Spriton

HOMETOWN:
Sami Thicket

Naia's companion, Kylan, is a Spriton song teller. Talented with both the lute and *firca*, he is often out of place among his more athletic friends. He is friendly and compassionate, though most of his knowledge comes from legends and song and not from experience. However physically awkward he is, his skill in song is unparalleled. With his *firca*, he is able to dream-stitch—attach dreamfasted memories to physical objects. This ability allows him to perform mystical feats, including sending dreamfasted messages, performing funerary rituals, and perhaps even more . . .

GELFLING FUNERALS

There are many rituals the Gelfling perform for their dead, but every clan's tradition includes burial. In this way, the Gelfling are returned to Thra. Kylan is well versed in many of these Gelfling rituals, including those of Gelfling long past that were preserved through song.

Kylan is the hero of the *Dark Crystal* young adult tie-in novel *Song of the Dark Crystal*.

REK'YR AND BENNU

CLAN:
Dousan

HOMETOWN:
The Wellspring

Rek'yr is a sandmaster—a Dousan captain. He is a bit of a rebel, confident and charming. Underlying his outgoing attitude, however, Rek'yr also has a deep respect for the cycle that is life and death. As a Dousan sandmaster, he knows that in the Crystal Desert, the weather and the environment are unpredictable and unforgiving, and that nothing should be taken for granted. The eloquent contemplations scattered amongst his otherwise nonchalant presentation hint at his much more critical and deep-running outlook on the world.

Rek'yr and his small crew travel the sands of the Crystal Desert aboard their Crystal Skimmer, Bennu. Bennu is one of the Dousan's most reliable Crystal Skimmers, quick and brave. Crystal Skimmers are native to the Crystal Desert and use their enormous fins to ride on the hot air currents that roll across the sand dunes.

REK'YR AND BREA

A bone necklace might be a strange gift to receive, but when it's coming from someone as mysterious and charismatic as Rek'yr, who wouldn't be flattered? Rek'yr's charms are difficult to deny, and even Brea can't help but notice his poetic way of discussing the more profound natures of Thra. Rian and Hup have noticed, too—and they don't like it one bit.

Before the Skeksis, Gelfling were peaceful. Hardworking. Playful. Knew how to cultivate the fruits of the earth and tame the creatures of the wood. They were one with Thra and one with one another! Seven clans. Seven voices singing the same song.

The Skeksis looked at the seven Gelfling clans and feared their unity. At the same time, they feared the connection the Gelfling had with the Crystal. To maintain power over the Crystal and Thra, the Skeksis orchestrated a wide-reaching plan to keep the Gelfling weak: Drive rifts of suspicion and rivalry among the seven clans and hide the Crystal away for safekeeping. As the clans fractured, the Skeksis favored the northern Vapra and named their Maudra the "All-Maudra"—leader of the other Maudras, thus placing the Vapra at the head of the six other clans. So began the Skeksis' hold over the seven clans.

THE SEVEN GELFLING CLANS AND THE MAUDRAS

ALL-MAUDRA MAYRIN AND THE VAPRA

HOMETOWN:
Ha'rar

REGION:
Northern Mountains

The most recent in a long succession of Vapran All-Maudras, All-Maudra Mayrin was groomed from a young age be the matriarch of the Vapra and all the Gelfling of Thra. In turn, she strives to pass on her diplomatic and political wisdom to her daughters. She both respects and fears the Skeksis, to whom she must report as their chosen Gelfling ambassador. In return, the Vapra bask in the favor of the Skeksis Lords, enjoying wealth and security in their mountainous home of Ha'rar.

The industrious Vapra benefit not only from the Skeksis' favor, but also from the vast natural resources available to them by way of the Silver Sea and the mountains surrounding Ha'rar. They are skilled metalworkers, both practical and ornamental. Many of the Vapra are also literate, a rarity among Gelfling, and frequent the labyrinthine Vapran library.

Mayrin places the safety of the Vapra above all, though she takes her role as All-Maudra seriously. When she realizes that Gelfling of all the seven clans are at risk, she knows immediately the dangerous path that must be taken.

ALL-MAUDRA MAYRIN AND BREA

Mayrin, an experienced Maudra, often tires of Brea's youthful and perhaps naive sense of justice. Mayrin has accepted Skeksis gifts for many trine, even at the expense of her Vapran constituents—and has, in many ways, become accustomed to it. When Brea begins taking things into her own hands, despite her mother's wishes, Mayrin must either turn a blind eye to her own shortcomings—or face them, and try to make herself into the mother and All-Maudra that Brea believes she could be.

ALL-MAUDRA MAYRIN AND THE SKEKSIS

Mayrin understands her position as All-Maudra is precarious and not to be taken for granted. She suspects the Skeksis' positioning of the Vapra was a strategy to cause strife and rivalry among the seven clans, but she has also grown to appreciate the trappings of their favor. She also knows that disobeying the Skeksis could put her clan—and perhaps all the Gelfling—in danger.

PALADINS

The Paladins, led by Princess Tavra, protect Ha'rar and its Citadel, as well as accompany trade caravans heading south to the other Gelfling clans. Many are skilled fencers and Landstrider riders, and those with wings are particularly adept at airborne operations.

MAUDRA FARA AND THE STONEWOOD

HOMETOWN:
Stone-in-the-Wood

REGION:
Endless Forest

Proud Maudra Fara leads her clan in mighty Stone-in-the-Wood, a village in the Endless Forest not too distant from the Castle of the Crystal. Maudra Fara believes in strength and loyalty, and will do whatever she believes is necessary for the good of her clan.

Though Ha'rar may be the Skeksis-ordained capital of the Gelfling world, Maudra Fara's central Stone-in-the-Wood is full of life and the songs of heroes current and long past. She is usually attended by Baffi, her pet Fizzgig.

Because Stone-in-the-Wood is so close to the Skeksis' castle, Stonewood are often called upon to serve as guards on the castle grounds. This prestige, in addition to the wealth of resources provided by the Endless Forest, has allowed the Stonewood to thrive and flourish. Unfortunately, it has also left a competitive streak among these forest-dwelling Gelfling—one that neighboring clans are quick to notice in their occasional rivalries.

MAUDRA FARA AND RIAN

Although Maudra Fara is the matriarch of Rian's clan, she is also a tenured Maudra who has lived near the Skeksis for many trine. When she finds that Rian may be a traitor and is sought by the Skeksis, she decides to put her clan before the individual, handing Rian over to Captain Ordon in the hopes it will solve the problem.

MAUDRA FARA AND SELADON

When Seladon declares herself All-Maudra upon the death of her mother, Mayrin, Maudra Fara voices her doubt that Seladon will be strong enough to resist the Skeksis. Maudra Fara and Seladon challenge each other to a duel in a Trial by Air to determine who will become the new matriarch of the seven clans.

THE CRUCIBLE

At the center of Stone-in-the-Wood is a monument called the Crucible, which also serves as the Stonewood clan's hearth. After battle, the Stonewood Gelfling discard their weapons into the Crucible, which burns with an everlasting flame. This ritual symbolizes leaving the violence of war in the past. Hundreds of swords and spears have been deposited into the Crucible over many trine.

MAUDRA ARGOT AND THE GROTTAN

HOMETOWN:
Domrak

REGION:
Caves of Grot

Maudra Argot is the oldest living Maudra. An unstoppable adventurer in her youth, she traveled topside many times and joined the Stonewood in battle against the Arathim. Many trine later, her sight has gone and her body is not as agile—but she is still unstoppable when it comes to taking new challenges head-on. Feisty and sharp-witted, she leads the reclusive Grottan clan with blunt advice punctuated with the sharp tapping of her cane. Aware that the other Gelfling look down upon the Grottan, Maudra Argot makes it a priority to encourage and protect her clan, teaching them to draw strength from Thra, and from within.

The Grottan clan live in Domrak, a Gelfling village hidden inside the rocky Caves of Grot. There, they spend most of their time maintaining the caves, gardening, and tending to the creatures that live in the surrounding tunnels, crevices, and ravines. Reasons to leave the caves are few and far between, and when a Grottan does leave, it must always be done at night. The bright light of the three suns hurts their eyes, which are adapted to living in near and total darkness.

MAUDRA ARGOT AND DEET

Maudra Argot cares about all the Grottan of her clan, though she has a special fondness for Deet. After Deet receives the vision from the Sanctuary Tree about what is happening outside of Grot, Maudra Argot sends Deet to the daylight world above. She can only hope Deet's curiosity and kindness will keep her safe during the dangerous journey.

MAUDRA LAESID AND THE DRENCHEN

HOMETOWN:
Great Smerth

REGION:
Swamp of Sog

Maudra Laesid is the hard-talking Drenchen leader, and the mother of Gurjin and Naia. While she has earned the trust of her clan with her no-nonsense, stubborn attitude, living in the distant Swamp of Sog has left her out of touch with the rest of the world. But the one thing Maudra Laesid is not out of touch with are her children. When she hears the rumors that Rian and Gurjin have betrayed the Skeksis, she does not hesitate to side with her son, and sends her daughter Naia to find and redeem him.

The Drenchen live deep in the Swamp of Sog, in a village encircling an ancient tree called Great Smerth. At home in both the canopy and the peaty bog, they are skilled rope workers and bola throwers. They are also the only Gelfling with gills that allow them to breathe underwater, and they have smaller wings that are used more frequently as fins than for flying.

MAUDRA ETHRI
AND THE SIFA

HOMETOWN:
Cera-Na

REGION:
Sifa Coast

Maudra Ethri became Maudra of the seafaring Sifa clan only a few trine ago, making her the youngest of the current Maudras. She is spiritual and intuitive, relying on her Sifan Far-Dreamers to guide her decisions—a practice not greatly effective when dealing with the Skeksis. She captains the Sifan clanship, the *Omerya*, an enormous vessel made of living coral. Given the chance, she would readily take her clan and sail away from the mainland to escape the Skeksis.

The Sifa clan can be found in small envoys sailing the Silver Sea and Sifa Coast. During important seasons and occasions, they gather in the port of Cera-Na. The Sifa are free-spirited and courageous. Despite their adventurous nature, they can also be overly superstitious. They do not like to remain in one place for long, and are quick to find reasons to depart. Despite their often ephemeral nature, the Sifa are one of the only clans willing to accept Gelfling of other clans into their society. Provided a Gelfling has the wherewithal to survive a fast-paced life aboard a Sifan ship, anyone is welcome.

MAUDRA SEETHI
AND THE DOUSAN

HOMETOWN:
The Wellspring

REGION:
Crystal Desert

Maudra Seethi is the matriarch of the Dousan, leading her nomadic clan with the help of several sandmaster captains. She is quiet and ageless, preferring to listen rather than to speak, and to perceive rather than to judge. Maudra Seethi takes her role of passing on the legacy of Gelfling funerary rites seriously. As the Dousan are rarely gathered in one place, this means relying on a close-knit group of apprentices called sandmasters, who bear the will and authority of their Maudra when she is unable to attend events in person.

The Dousan travel the Crystal Desert aboard their Crystal Skimmers, seeking wisdom and enlightenment within the vast and changing sands. In difficult times, or when called by the sandmaster council and Maudra Seethi, the Dousan gather at the Wellspring, a verdant oasis deep in the Crystal Desert.

MAUDRA MERA
AND THE SPRITON

HOMETOWN:
Sami Thicket

REGION:
Spriton Plains

The traditional and shrewd Maudra Mera looks after the Spriton from Sami Thicket, a village nestled in a small wood in the middle of the Spriton Plains. Maudra Mera's approach to tending her clan begins with enthusiastic loyalty to the Skeksis, in exchange for the blessing of their resources and protection. She will do anything to keep her clan safe.

While most make their home in Sami Thicket, the Spriton Gelfling spend much of their time traveling to trade in Stone-in-the-Wood, the Castle of the Crystal, and sometimes as far north as Ha'rar. They are knowledgeable in agriculture and creature husbandry, as well as textile creation and other fine arts.

The Castle of the Crystal. The fortress that holds captive the Heart of Thra. And in that castle, the Skeksis Lords wait and maintain their possession of that which they have stolen.

THE SKEKSIS AND THE MYSTICS

SKEKSO THE EMPEROR

Seizing power and taking the throne as ruler of the Skeksis Lords requires a brutal vigor that only skekSo has. Though he may have once enjoyed the fawning adoration of the Gelfling, that high has long faded. Now, the Emperor lives only to further his own ends: to keep the terrible power he has usurped over Thra and the Dark Crystal.

Emperor skekSo is cruel, selfish, and supremely intelligent. He is painfully aware that the other lords would betray him and usurp his power given the chance. Thus, the Emperor's alertness to the constant scheming of his underlings has transformed into an overpowering paranoia, causing him to trust no one but himself. Vehement that he will never lose his position as Emperor, skekSo pursues youth and strength—masterfully executing every and any action necessary to keep his scepter in his hand and the other Skeksis at his feet. With the power of the Dark Crystal, he will never become dust!

Emperor skekSo is tall and agile, no stranger to the battlefield or the physical demands of war. But his intimidating appearance and grand, self-important speeches hide a terrible secret. Beneath his metal armor, his body is weak and crumbling, succumbing to the corruption brought on him by his fixation on the darkening. It is only a matter of time before the other Skeksis discover this, but the Emperor is determined to solve the issue with Gelfling Essence before his weakness is revealed.

THE EMPEROR AND RIAN

In the beginning, skekSo paid no mind to the names and faces of the Gelfling guards who worked within the Castle of the Crystal. But once Rian fled the castle with the Skeksis' secret, threatening to spread the truth far and wide, Emperor skekSo certainly took note. The Emperor knows Rian will become the champion of the Gelfling resistance—and so he must be stopped, by any means necessary.

THE EMPEROR AND THE GELFLING

The Emperor may have been content to allow the Gelfling to exist so long as they remained subservient to him and the Skeksis, but Rian and his friends are putting all of that at risk. The only reason the Emperor does not immediately decide to eradicate the Gelfling is because he does not want to eliminate the source of his new favorite substance: life-giving Gelfling Essence.

SKEKSIL THE CHAMBERLAIN

Once the Emperor's most trusted advisor, skekSil the Chamberlain's duty among the Skeksis is to maintain the Emperor's personal assets, from his Podling servants to his daily wardrobe. Despite his seeming loyalty to the Emperor during his impossibly long tenure, it is no secret among the Skeksis that the Chamberlain is actually among the most scheming and manipulative of them all. While he may seem to confide in and trust his fellow Skeksis, this is just a front to gain their confidence and get what he wants; in the end, the only person the Chamberlain trusts is the Chamberlain.

While he may have the same appetite for power as the other Skeksis, the Chamberlain's sense of self-preservation may be slightly stronger. Accordingly, he prefers to do his dealing out of sight and from the shadows. If no one knows the Chamberlain is behind the machinations that keep the Skeksis' powers shifting, then no one can stop him—and if someone else can take the fall for his actions while he continues to benefit, all the better.

The Chamberlain may disappear on the sidelines when he wishes not to be seen, but when he makes his entrance, all in the room can't help but notice his signature high-pitched whimper. His robes are typically red and black; well-kept and regal, as his own appearance is one of the Chamberlain's highest-tier priorities.

THE EMPEROR AND THE CHAMBERLAIN

The Chamberlain has long enjoyed his spot at the Emperor's right hand, managing his affairs and other sensitive matters. But when the Chamberlain failed to apprehend Rian, and the Gelfling rebellion began to rise out of hand, the Emperor turned away from the Chamberlain's "light-touch" machinations. Falling out of the Emperor's favor was a shock the Chamberlain was not ready to handle, hurling him into a long upward scramble to regain the position that was once solidly his.

SKEKVAR THE GENERAL

skekVar the General's main priorities were once the maintenance of the castle defense forces, but after the Gelfling began to rebel, his propensity toward brute violence brought him into the Emperor's favor. Contrary to the Chamberlain's approach of manipulating the Gelfling into remaining fragmented and subservient, the General believes violent force is all that is necessary to control the rising rebellion.

Towering as a mountain and just as dense, the General's presence is always felt in his thunderous footsteps and booming voice. He is always one to throw his weight around, physically and figuratively, especially since he has no particular talent for words. Fists and swords and other bludgeoning weapons are the General's language, in which he is monstrously fluent.

The Chamberlain and the General

Confronted with the uprising of the Gelfling and in the wake of the Chamberlain's failure to quell the seemingly inevitable rebellion, the General's brute-force strategy begins to win the Emperor's ear. For the first time, the General finds himself a rising star—finally, the other Skeksis begin to hear the promise in his simple and time-tested advice! But if any Skeksis is not to be crossed, it is the Chamberlain . . .

SKEKTEK
THE SCIENTIST

skekTek's unparalleled technical and intellectual prowess is thanks to both his obsessive personality and his lack of moral inhibitions. He will go to any length to develop his diabolical inventions, most of which probe into the nature of darkness and the transference of life energy from one creature to another. The range and depth of his disturbing experiments are proof of his heartlessness in regard to the feelings and lives of other living things.

The Scientist harbors a not-so-secret belief that he is the smartest of all the Skeksis. Even smarter than the Emperor. But intelligence alone will never carry him to the top, and so skekTek applies his knowledge and technical skill across hundreds of projects, hoping to establish his worth to the Emperor and maintain his position among the Skeksis Lords.

The Scientist's prowess is intellectual, not physical. He has a narrow figure and is actually quite weak compared to his bulkier cohorts. Acutely aware of his shortcomings, he has already engineered artificial improvements for himself. After losing his eye, he developed and installed a superior, mechanical one for himself.

THE SCIENTIST AND THE CHAMBERLAIN

The Scientist wants nothing more than to have the freedom to perform his experiments in his lab as he pleases, and the Chamberlain recognizes this. As long as the two stay out of each other's way, they are willing to work together to get what they want. But as soon as the Emperor's favor is at stake—not to mention Gelfling Essence—all bets are off.

SKEKZOK THE RITUAL MASTER

skekZok the Ritual Master cares not for the day-to-day politics of the Skeksis court, and neither does he care about the Gelfling aside from the Essence that can be extracted from them. But as soon as the rites and rituals of punishment are involved, the Ritual Master's sadistic character comes to life. His eagerness to deliver punishment is not restricted to carrying out such rites on Gelfling; in fact, he may show even more enthusiasm when it comes to settling scores among his fellow Skeksis.

Despite his strictness, the Ritual Master is no stranger to bending the rules to his advantage. When beholding other Skeksis going against the grain—or the Emperor's wishes—the Ritual Master is no meek informant. He is much more likely to withhold his knowledge and use it for extortion.

The Ritual Master is often the figurehead of poise, upright and well-dressed for every occasion. He carries a scepter with which he officiates his many proceedings, and is fond of gold, as it represents the regal power and wealth with which he believes he is imbued.

SKEKLACH THE COLLECTOR

Materialistic and covetous, skekLach the Collector's main duty among the Skeksis is to collect the tithes from the Gelfling clans—though by the time she and her entourage return to the castle with the Gelfling offerings, many of the shiniest and most precious pretties have mysteriously gone missing, later appearing conveniently within the Collector's hoard-like treasure troves. The only thing that makes the Collector happier than receiving a gift is the opportunity to seize one by force.

The Collector is just as prone to *collecting* upon her corporeal body as she is to hoarding material items. Her face and skin are swollen with putrescence, perhaps the outward expression of her vile spirit and personality. Because of her very visible physical ailments, the Collector wants to obtain all the youth-restoring Essence she can drink.

SKEKOK THE SCROLL-KEEPER

skekOk the Scroll-Keeper's role is to keep the records of the Skeksis' rule over Thra, and because this duty fell to such a dishonest character, the records always show what skekOk—or his Skeksis benefactors—want them to show. The history of the Skeksis has been rewritten countless times to reflect well on skekOk or any of his cohorts who paid him in wealth or compliments. Among the Skeksis, skekOk is not the most dangerous in battle, but one can be sure the account of the confrontation will shine favorably on him no matter the real outcome.

The Scroll-Keeper is not as girthy as many of the other Skeksis, and wears a collection of spectacles upon his narrow snout. He has a limited amount of white, thinning hair, something he is rather proud of, considering many of the other lords have long gone bald.

skekAyuk the Gourmand's hunger and gluttony are not restricted to mere food, though satisfying his infinite appetite is certainly of prime concern for this boisterous, vicious Skeksis. His role within the Skeksis order is to orchestrate the many courses required for every feasting event, as well as to prepare and deliver the Emperor's personal meals when requested. The Gourmand prefers carnivorous meals and enjoys the process of slaughtering creatures for consumption. And if a meal involves eating a critter alive—even better.

The Gourmand's lust for fine cuisine and the other pleasures of life may stem from a deep-seated fear of mortality. After all, no amount of feeding ever seems to quiet the deep fear in his gut. When faced with the Gelfling uprising, the Gourmand—perhaps more than the other Skeksis—reacts with sheer panic. Paired with his hulking size, this terror transformed into rage makes the Gourmand one of the most dangerous Skeksis to face during battle.

SKEKEKT THE ORNAMENTALIST

skekEkt the Ornamentalist is responsible, for the appearance of the Skeksis' rule, from the design of the castle to the garments and headdresses worn by the Skeksis themselves. She is especially fond of garments made from the furs, feathers, and skins of other creatures, believing those to be the most decadent and luxurious.

The appearance of power and youth is paramount to skekEkt, so although she hungers for vital Essence, she also believes the Chamberlain's approach to manipulating the Gelfling is more befitting of a Skeksis Lord. She will never be caught acting like a savage beast . . . unless it really does become necessary!

skekMal the Hunter's thirst for pure violence and terror is unequaled even among the power-hungry Skeksis Lords. skekMal lives for the thrill of the hunt and savors the carnage of the kill. He collects trophies from his more challenging conquests, though until the Gelfling uprising, there was hardly a creature in Thra that was challenging *enough*.

Outside of the hunt, skekMal has few pastimes. He rarely makes appearances in the court of the Skeksis, as most of the other lords—while loath to admit it—fear the Hunter's unpredictable, violent nature. Only the Emperor is said to be able to control him.

While hunting, skekMal wears a bone mask to hide his Skeksis face. His speed and unmatched silence make him virtually invisible, especially at night. For many trine, his true identity as a Skeksis Lord was unknown—he was merely called the Hunter by Gelfling and Podlings throughout the Endless Forest and the surrounding region.

RIAN AND THE HUNTER

skekMal has never lost a mark once he has been set on the trail. But just as he is about to kill Rian, the Chamberlain gets in the way! This is the first time the Hunter has ever lost his prey, sending him into a furious fixation that can only be sated by the Stonewood's blood.

URVA THE ARCHER

urVa the Archer is an urRu, or Mystic, a peaceful race with a mysterious connection to the Skeksis. Whatever happens to one happens to the other; each pair represents two halves of some ancient whole.

The Archer is no different. urVa's powerful foresight and ability to see the forest for the trees makes him one of the most intuitive and active Mystics. While he bears none of the bloodlust of his Skeksis counterpart, skekMal the Hunter, he still exhibits many of the same skills in seeking that which is difficult to find. The Archer is methodical and practical, using his superior senses and tracking abilities to locate the elusive Aughra and aid her in awakening the Gelfling resistance.

THE HUNTER AND THE ARCHER

The Hunter and the Archer both pursue their goals without rest. Whatever they are after, they will find. However, where skekMal is fixated on sating his corporeal desires, the Archer has mastered the art of letting go. He is prepared to surrender to destiny in the name of a greater good, if the need should ever arise . . .

SKEKGRA THE HERETIC

Hundreds of trine ago, skekGra was known as the Conqueror, the most dangerous and unforgiving of all the Skeksis. He obeyed skekSo's command and set the Skeksis flag upon every mountaintop, fearlessly destroying whatever and whomever might try to stop him.

But battle and victory did not heal the aching in his heart. He came to remember a time before he was the Conqueror—before he was a Skeksis. He remembered when he was one with his urRu half—when he was *whole*. When he voiced his desire to become *one* once again, the Emperor and the other Skeksis were enraged and horrified. They cast him out the Castle of the Crystal, and the Emperor gave him a new name: the Heretic.

The Heretic's fixation on merging with his Mystic half has manifested in many ways over the many hundreds of trine since leaving the castle. After finally finding urGoh the Wanderer, the Heretic allowed his focus to shift, pouring all his efforts into making sure the fates would align and allow him to merge with urGoh. This included leaving a series of clues that would help the Gelfling end Skeksis rule and reunite the Skeksis and the Mystics.

urGoh
the WANDERER

The way of the Mystics is to be detached from the world and the events that unfold within it, to watch but not touch, and to perceive without deigning to *know*. urGoh the Wanderer was unable to subscribe to that philosophy. Like the other Mystics, he never stayed in one place long, a temporary visitor to the many regions of Thra.

Yet the other Mystics would, in time, return to the Valley where their Master waited, while the Wanderer's returns became fewer and farther between. urGoh wandered through the woods and the mountains and the Crystal Desert in search of what might heal the feeling of incompleteness. What he found was skekGra the Heretic, his Skeksis half.

The Wanderer is an absentminded character, possibly because of his fondness for mood- and mind-expanding substances. He wanders now through the endless landscape of the mind, dreaming of the joy it will be when he is finally one with his Skeksis counterpart.

THE WANDERER AND THE HERETIC

The Wanderer and the Heretic now spend all their days together in the Circle of the Suns, a mysterious and ruined place hidden somewhere in the Crystal Desert. There, they travel unstoppably down a path that both the Mystics and the Skeksis consider forbidden: to know the future and to influence it, and to use that power to reunite the Mystics and the Skeksis once again.

OTHERS

Ah! But it is not just Gelfling who live in Thra, and who defend it. And who attack it. The world is full of minds and hearts and voices.

PODLINGS

Some Podlings even have the honor of working with Aughra!

No matter where one visits in Thra, one will always find Podlings. They live close to the earth, both literally and figuratively. Their culture is typically warm and welcoming, and they often live in close proximity to Gelfling, trading in produce and fine crafts. Although the Podlings speak their own language, many have also learned to speak Gelfling in order to better draw their two races closer together.

PODLING SERVANTS

Many Podlings live and some work in the Castle of the Crystal. Some serve in the kitchens preparing the Gourmand's endless banquets. Any Podlings with musical talents are required to play in the Skeksis' Podling band in the Emperor's throne room.

AUGHRA'S ATTENDANT

This Podling is the latest in a long line of Aughra's assistants, a hereditary occupation that has been passed down through the generations. Although his days are long and thankless, he takes his job very seriously—even if sometimes it can be difficult.

ARATHIM

One of the most ancient races of Thra, the Arathim are a broad family of multi-legged arthropod creatures. Their subspecies are innumerous, ranging in size and number of legs. Despite the large variance in physical appearance, all Arathim are part of a singular hive mind called the Ascendency.

The Arathim once controlled much of the land now inhabited by the Gelfling. During the First Arathim Wars, they lost much of their home territory and were forced to retreat into the cavernous regions near and below the Endless Forest. But do not be fooled. Though they lost to the Gelfling and the Skeksis in the wars, the Arathim are anything but defeated.

SILK SPITTERS

Silk Spitters are among the largest of the Arathim species. In fact, there is no known limit to the size a Silk Spitter can reach. Called "Spitters" for short, these armored Arathim soldiers do well as solitary hunters and are devastating in groups. They get their name from the sticky strings of webbing they are able to produce, both to build their hives as well as to capture and restrain prey.

THREADERS

Threaders are much smaller than their Silk Spitter brethren, many small enough to hide within the folds of clothing or Gelfling architecture. Threaders have the uncanny ability to control the minds and bodies of the creatures they make contact with. While controlling their host, Threaders have a similar experience to Gelfling dreamfasting, able to see and hear their host's memories and thoughts.

THREADED TAVRA

After being captured by the Skeksis, Tavra was given to an Arathim Threader to infiltrate and ambush the Stonewood during their rebellion. Due to the length of time bonded with the Threader, it is unclear if Tavra can now survive without it.

MORE CREATURES OF THRA

Countless creatures inhabit the many regions of Thra, each suited to its environment. Thra is a wondrous place, where there are no distinct lines between animal and plant and mineral.

FIZZGIGS

GRUENAKS

These pitiable creatures were mostly eradicated many trine ago. Some survived and two were later captured by the Chamberlain to assist skekTek the Scientist in his lab. In order to prevent them from sharing the secrets, their lips have been sewn shut—they can never tell the Scientist that they actually work for the Chamberlain.

These furry, energetic critters native to the Endless Forest are often kept as pets—but only by those who are up to the challenge of their rambunctious nature. Wild Fizzgigs roll in small packs, while those kept domestically tend to be choosy about what other creatures share their space. Once a Fizzgig chooses an owner, they can become protective and loyal, making them a wise choice of companion for any Gelfling who travels alone.

LANDSTRIDERS

Perhaps some of the most versatile creatures to roam Thra, the long-legged Landstriders can be found everywhere from the rocky cliffs near Ha'rar all the way to the flat Spriton Plains. They are stubborn, intuitive, and intelligent creatures, and not easy to tame; thus, it takes a Gelfling of great skill and compassion to ride one.

Because of their long legs, Landstriders feed primarily on low-understory foliage, using their proboscises to drink nectar from flowering trees.

ARMALIGS

Prior to being trained to carry carriages by the Skeksis, Armaligs primarily lived underground. They made their burrows and colonies in the root networks of the trees within the Endless Forest. Now, most wild Armaligs are extinct, with the majority living in captivity within the Castle of the Crystal Armalig stables.

NURLOCS

Closely related to Armaligs, Nurlocs are an armored worm native to the Caves of Grot. While the babies are small and docile, Nurlocs become more obstinate as they grow older. Nurlocs that are fond of the Grottan Gelfling who feed and rear them may sometimes build their nests close to Gelfling passageways, creating inconvenient blockages.

UNAMOTHS

Considered sacred for their mysterious connection to Thra, Unamoths are native to the northern coasts near Ha'rar. The Imperial Unamoth is the totem animal of the Vapra clan. As larvae, they burrow in mountainsides and under tree bark to hide from the cold. Their pupal period is very long; although many Gelfling naturalists believe it to be dependent on temperature and exposure to moisture, no one has ever been able to reliably and consistently predict when an Unamoth will emerge from its chrysalis.

These flying creatures are used to send messages and items between Gelfling clans. They are obedient and goal-oriented critters, with both perfect memories and tireless stamina that allow them to travel quickly and without stop to any corner of Thra.

Deatea. Deratea. Kidakida. Arugaru . . .

And so the flames of hope burn. The fires of resistance! The Gelfling rise and the Skeksis tremble. Like a thousand stars in the dark sky, all bending across the cosmos to one point—to one day of reckoning—to the Great Conjunction.

Heroes of Thra—this is your legacy!